— FACT —

it real

this is

IT'S NOT ALL BAD

poetry is the new Rock n' roll (???) but I do respect realism

Paul Casey

— VERBAL WANK — SORRY

heaventree

IT'S NOT ALL BAD

First edition 2009
© Paul Casey 2009
All rights reserved.

ISBN 978-1-906038-37-3

Cover photograph: 'It's Not All Bad' © Anne-Marie Glasheen 2009

Heaventree logo design by Panna Chauhan

Published in the UK by
The Heaventree Press,
Institute for Creative Enterprise,
Puma Way,
Coventry Technology Park,
Coventry, UK
CV1 2TT

Printed by Prontaprint Coventry Ltd

We are grateful for the financial support of

CONTENTS

Scannánaigh the Poet   7

It's Not All Bad   14

An Béal Corcra   25

Scannánaigh the Poet

Scannánaigh the poet
one day traded
his pencil
for a lens
and his paper
for a reel

wrote these
new poems
eye-ear poems
poet-less poems

Scannánaigh the poet
one day sent his very eyes
into exile
into plots
to breathe
you see

Scannánaigh the poet
now swam in a new sea
of satire

iambic celluloid
anapaestic f-stop
dactylic actors
an alliteration
of lighting and
a versification
of visions

Scannánaigh the poet
was in a very

different sea
of sound effects
of irony

a sea
of modern prosody
of new closed forms

ask Petrarchan Scannánaigh
for a modern sunrise sonnet
and you'll receive

When aiming camera just make sure to think
That all the mise-en-scène is balanced well
That all the actors have their lines to tell
That shades and hues and shadows are in sync

When if you need your players not to blink
To shield their eyes from sun's own jealous yell
To fan and nudge their egos to excel
Make sure to look as if you're on the brink

Of breaking through to poetry unseen
Of bringing through the actor's greatest day
Of culminating new creations dreamed

For when the thespian instinct will not play
Suspects the charioteer about to fold
The last word of each line is never told

Ask too of Scannánaigh
an ancient anamorphic quatorzain
and he'll smile in plain and say another
sonnet, two tercets two quatrains

8

opus historium, Clio hysterium
ask laboured Scannánaigh
while placing a prop
a limerick to requite
and he'll recite

There was an old actor from yore
Who thought that to film was a bore
Till he moved all his grace
From his hands to his face
And entered the stage nevermore

Scannánaigh the poet
was in a completely
different sea
of emotion and
morality

ask him for
a villanelle and
he'll answer with five tercets
and a set-dressing quatrain

I found a poet in me
And sighed when me he saw
An artist finally free

The road to mastery
A softened cheerful paw
I found a poet in me

Unravelling mystery
With feathered forms a-claw
An artist finally free

I now could speak with tree
Have arguments with flaw
I found a poet in me

To flee or not to flee
A danger to the law
An artist finally free

It's best I climb a tree
There with the crows I'll caw
I found a poet in me
An artist finally free

cinquain
sextain
rondel
rondeau
roundel
rondeau redoublé

un triolet aussi

Asked for a haiku
Swift sun surgeon-shining seas
Ninety-page screenplay

a movement and a motion
Scannánaigh the poet
was worrying now
in a very
different sea
of symbols
and imagery

a sea
of newly dreamed cities
of new open forms

of scripted coblas
ad-lib odes
couplet cameos
a rhyming montage
of troubadouric
flashbacks
of scheduled epigrams
and filtered ballads

delirious Scannánaigh the poet
was panicking now
in this completely
different simile sea

terza rima shutter speeds
pantoum close-ups
virelai ancien
clapperboards
continuity ballades
virelai nouveau
light meters
and focus-pulling glose

onomatopoeic stampeding crowds
new phonetic zoomings
homoeoprophoron animal handlers
make-up consonance swindlers
and assonant stunt predictors
the rhythm and effect of
accelerating producers

sustaining
pie quebrado atmospheres

the phonetic rhetoric
of the assistant director
and talkie iteratio
of the walkie-talkie
lipograms and
inner dialogue synaloepha
of discernment
the caesura
of discretion

Scannánaigh the poet
staring at the
rhyming crew
and cast
at the
unrhyming entirety
simply
shook his head

rich rhyme
mirror rhyme
identity rhyme
virtual rhyme
endecasillabo
gallic decasyllable
alexandrines
iambic pentameter
all mercilessly
sent to the slaughter
of booms and gates
and gels and mics and

of avant-garde gung-ho
fame-spangled hot-heads

da da da
for the
nursery rhyme advocates

who lose
iambically, take ten
a trochaic action
anapaestically
it's a wrap
in the can
dactylic filmistry
an amphibraic filtration
of spondaic faux pas
and pyrrhic edits

Scannánaigh's stress patterns
and tightrope metres
designer syllables
all lost
drowned
realised Scannánaigh
the poet
by the conquering
camera
and the seventh
art

(Scannánaigh (pronounced Ska-Naa-Ni): in Irish, to film)

It's not all bad

I saw that devil again
On the TV today
Preaching away.
Didn't have much to say
Looking around for prey
I didn't stay.

But what to do, what to do?
The feeling next, was wonder
Which hit me like a ton of down
So much cannot be uttered, I thought,
With thunder.
Some veiled focus, just out of sight
A mixture of desires
I close my ears to faeries
Earth-seed cures my ires
While colours, form, clarity and pep
Re-form with every step

Invented, for what else to do
Are these endeavours
While burning deeper still
Untouchable will.
I run to the emptiness
To the layers of joy
Life's eternal gifts
Unknowable still
Like Troy.

The eye that opens while full
Is often under fire.
What must yet be done or said

Or sought?
What creatures are these who discover
Such sufficient meaning in wealth?
The very same who slash with smiles and cast
That 'blissful' defence
The very same, inhuman,
Who cause us not to rest.

What days are these surrounding?
What bird would choose this plight?
These laws of men are drowning,
What is there left to fight?
The freedoms gained are heavy-light.
Heavy-light freedoms gained.
To know or not to know
To care or feel or think?
I run from absinthe
I run for tomorrow
I run to her.
Free from napalm-mustard hate
Free for another day
Free to try, to be.

It's said before you die
Your whole life flashes by.
I open my eye,
And time, compressed, defiant,
Flashes everything by
At once.
All left is that emerald question
Caught, trapped in a seeking eye
Like a stone in your custard,
Shocking, breaking, unwanted.

So where is this talent of mine?
This thing that drives me?
This thing which drives me lightward,
Onward, madward, saneward?
What is this seeking thing?
This elusive, swimming will?
Which mocks and jeers in delight
At the confusion of this plight.
Stories within. Lonely. And joyful.
Dreams about me. Wishful. Tearful.
And I, thoughtful.

Antennae of the mind
Stretch outward again and find
Those angels and devils alike
Spectators of my life.

My life?
The PC, TV, lingo, muso,
Celluloid, free-flight Gringo.
Bohemian strings from a poet's wings.
Awakening Phoenix, Chinese whiskey,
Snowboard, free-fall fancy.
African eagle, English beagle
Real Irish Regal.
Frugal, bourgeoisie thought-machine.
A seller of salesman
A suer of suers
A Killer of whims of such naïve drinkers of Pimms
Number One
Or number ten of 6 billion odd.
How many of them can be numbers?
Five-sevenths of a mathematician?
Lest Titan fly out from Saturn's lure,

Let these numbers float like clouds, and endure.
Lest Charon stop her flirting tango,
Let these numbers try the fandango.
'Number One indeed', said Lucifer, that dreary sun,
'And you'll be number Two, Yes? Done?'
To which I needs reply, 'Not this eye.'

My life?
Plato's promise. Nietzsche's betrayal. Foucault's ambition.
A ring on Joyce's finger. A flea on Yeats' balls.
A knife in the Taoiseach's halls.
A boule without insurance.
A boat with spoon-sized oars

Why does grime sound like crime?
Or fame like flame?
Pallbearers of the wicked, beware the same.
And shame, that weighty hurdle,
Curdling the words of those sheepish herds.
Lights please! Perfection's flaw is revealed!
The perfect inclusion
In that imperfect emerald
'Is ignored', says Ann
My blue-eyed faerie
In a daydream, mind you,
So the words may still be mine.
But no mind.
I have enough freckles to remember,
That although the sun is blinding,
In sips the light is kinder
The seeking ear will find her
That answer to unbind her.

Is it really all that bad?

With so much to be had?
Can it really be so sad?
Invasion is a fad.

Just what is it we eat these days?
In this maze, this haze of the age?
Your taste-buds should remind you ...
The TV wars, didactic bores
Information stores, cultural sores
Closing doors, ethnic gores
Fly-faced poors on all fours
Scores of land-mined floors
And the greedy roars of armchair whores.
And what wine to wash this down?
Hijack fears, chemical beers, 7 o'clock seers,
Crocodile tears, Typtronic gears, new-world years,
Bush & Blair peers,
Uneducated hetero-sexual Queers
With paradoxical rears
And mighty spears
Like garden shears.

Is it really all that bad?
With so much to be had?
Could it truly be so mad?
Isn't life just like a tadpole?

With a free thesaurus.
An added chorus too.

Is it really all that bad?
With so much to be had?
Evolution and ages still go by
It's rad.

We have stored, spored and floored,
The faerie Ann nearby, with sword,
Oared and all.
Ann the prophetic faerie,
Tying higher worlds of blue
Returns with a warning, hued in blue.

'What's inside them now, PC?
What's your audience going through?
I dropped the sword years ago you twit!
I haven't seen the sight of it.'

'Well what's that glinting in your hand then?', says I.

'That's my sense of humour you eejit!', says she.
'The audience think YOU'RE going to decapitate them, not me!'

'Ah toddle off!', says I.
'Can I get back to my poem now?'

Anyhow.
That's what it's about my friend,
It's every moment you meet,
Every second you greet,
Have dinner for six and some wine.
Put on some Schubert.
Be fine.
Who's a poet's ass anyway?
Go on, even you say,
'Stop fucking around, assholes of the world,
All the good things are beyond your reach anyway,
Assholes of the world.'
Cos We, new-aged, ethic-sussed

Jazz-basted ghosts of jargon
Are checking you out.
Just to C.
Those eyebrows may fail you
Politics of the day
Politics of the person
Politics of the culture
Hairstyle of the day
The French foreign legion for God's sake.
Art and Politics?
Where will it all end?
Well let me mention a thing or two.

The times we're in are delicate days,
Crystal worlds of compromise are these
More books and films and music
Than the brow could ever read or heed
Rain is a rarity or rain is the norm
But what difference?
As long as we survive this storm
For in its eye, the whispered promise
Of a better form.

And so as we row, with spoons in full flow
On to those shores and open doors
Without TV wars
No roaring whores or icy floors
We know
Those winds of envy may yet blow
As even I, a mere crow
Still keep this extra claw
That blushing poe
That emerald flaw
That sea-green glow

Twisted hoe
Poe in stow
We know
Those winds of greed will still blow
And so
On we go
What do we really know?

Is it really all that bad?
Aren't we often enough glad?
Don't you love it, just a tad,
This global village pad?

American-Jap-Chinese-Euro-Afro whateverisms
UN, equity, union, oil-based people-prisms
Ice-cream cones and trippy seventies sepia
Roller-coaster ride visions
Buckle down those hides
Doesn't it seem just too much sometimes?
This is not the wrong question.
Thank God for digestion.

How else to escape these coy indictments?
How else to arrest these hoi-polloi infringements?
Singeing arrangements of opportunistic verisimilitude?
Trying to con I?
Lest we forget
Necromancy and illusion manipulation
Are an ancient game.
See-through just the same.
The ignorant will maim.
Hardly an itch, to this flame.
Not a paying spectator in this life
This amphitheatre is full

Of peanut gallery chirps
And second-hand burps
This amphitheatre of the imagination.

Carpé Philos! Seize the Love.
Carpé pomme-frites
Al dente.
Can't pay the rent, eh?
Haven't got a cent, eh?
Those anti-poet pomme-frites will tell you,
That might is actually right.
What a fright!
A sight for sore rights, quite.
POMME FRITES SHITE!!
Telling me how to shed my light.
This moment feels tight.
Tense, but not trite.
Undo this mental blight!
It's a warning to politicians and the like,
Not to touch a poet's right
For you shall rediscover night
That lumberjack of might
And yet it seems we share some light
But I've caught a different flight
A rhyming delight
This emerald of sight
My very own bright white height.

Corruptions of the world beware
This earth remembers more treasures
Than you could dare
And she's rarely fair
To those who tear.

Is it nearly all that bad?

We have therapists for the mad
We have prisons for the bad
Hope for the post-grad
Awards for the best ad
Second chances for a wayward lad
Meaning for the pseudo-nomad
All this we've had.

In this short wisp of time I find
So many are truly kind
In truth, we're not too blind
We know the shape of Dylan's mind
And Oscar Wilde's behind
Or what he left behind
Not this
'I the I of I will ire I if this Kei, Thai,
20 000 Euro Khoi braai is too cheap to buy.'
I sigh
Our meaning is thickened by Phi.

A lover's sigh
Our anniversary is nigh
Without drugs and so very high
There is Hope, Faith's very daughter by
To light the way
Beneath war-obsessed fools
Missile-guided ghouls
This
'I am greater than thou in Hell.'
Eat your Hell
I'm very well Without that smell
The media fell into this ancient well
So I'll kiss and tell
For me you cannot sell
No matter how loud your bell.

It can only be that bad
If you think it's all that sad
If you feel that you've been had
Not just cos you don't like
Roquefort salade.

And so finally and with texture, if I may
Throw the rest of these words your way
Before I cause you some dismay
By owning too much of the day
Let me say
It's not all bad.

An Béal Corcra

delightful aftertaste
this river
of kingly colour
ocular delight
this stream
of purpoesy
a vein-aortic mix
of spirit liquid

as even
evolved vampires
overdose
on blends
of rich-thick
contradiction,
of unravelled
breaths expired

even as
seasoned muses
pilgrim-seasoned muses
each leave a trail
of purple dripping
from tongue and teeth
a new harvest
of mystery

and even as
starved poets sip
the mountain manna
purple poem wine,
dream-drunk poets

pulse-deafened
descend purply
their seasoned lips

(An Béal Corcra: in Irish, The purple mouth)